Stitching Dreams
The Inspiring Life of Herla Barthelemy

Stitching Dreams

The Inspiring Life of Herla Barthelemy

HERLA BARTHELEMY

Text Herla Barthelemy
Copyright © Herla Barthelemy

First print April 2025

CONTENTS

CHAPTER 1: THREADING THE NEEDLE OF DESTINY (AGES 1-20) — 7

CHAPTER 2: STITCHING A NEW LIFE IN AMERICA (AGES 21-30) — 19

CHAPTER 3: WEAVING SUCCESS: MY FASHION EMPIRE (AGES 30-50) — 29

CHAPTER 4: DESIGNING DREAMS: MY WORK WITH DISNEY (AGES 50-PRESENT) — 35

CHAPTER 5: STITCHING FAITH AND FAMILY — 43

CHAPTER 6: THREADS OF ADVENTURE: MY TRAVELS AND CULTURAL EXPERIENCES — 57

CHAPTER 7: THE ART OF BALANCE: MARTIAL ARTS AND WELLNESS — 71

CHAPTER 8: PRESERVING THE ART: MY LEGACY AND VISION FOR THE FUTURE — 77

CHAPTER 1: THREADING THE NEEDLE OF DESTINY (AGES 1-20)

Part I: Early Life in Haiti

The rhythmic hum of the sewing machine has been the soundtrack of my life for as long as I can remember. That steady mechanical purr, accompanied by the soft swish of fabric and the subtle click of scissors, forms a melody that has guided me from a small town in Haiti to the bustling streets of New York City and beyond. But long before I ever touched a sewing machine or threaded a needle, the seeds of my passion were already taking root in the vibrant, complex soil of my homeland.

I was born on March 20, 1948, in Port-au-Prince, Haiti. My father hailed from the coastal town of Belle Anse, while my mother's roots were in Croix-des-Missions. From the very beginning, I occupied a special place in my family as the firstborn child—a position of both privilege and responsibility that would shape the course of my life in ways I could never have imagined.

In Haitian culture, being the firstborn is very special. This wasn't just true in my immediate family but extended to my grandparents as well. I remember my grandmother from my father's side spoiling me, and my grandmother from my mother's side doing the same. This doting treatment from my grandmothers was more than just familial affection—it was a cultural tradition, a way of honoring the continuity of generations. This special status came with its own set of expectations and responsibilities, ones that I would grow into as I got older.

As the eldest of six children, four brothers and one sister, I quickly learned the importance of family and the interconnectedness of our lives. Little did I know then how crucial these early lessons would be in shaping my future.

The Haiti of my childhood was one of vibrant colors, rich flavors, and age-old traditions. Our daily life revolved around the rhythms of family, food, and community. The memories of those early years are still vivid in my mind, a kaleidoscope of sights, sounds, and especially tastes that I carry with me to this day.

I loved the Haitian foods as a child growing up and still do. Every day was a culinary adventure, with my family cooking the delicious Haitian cuisine that has become such an integral part of my identity. We had red beans, rice, and goat meat. But it wasn't just the dishes themselves that were special—it was the entire process of procuring and preparing our meals that made them so memorable.

In Haiti, the concept of "fresh" took on a whole new meaning. Every day my parents had maids that would go to the marketplace and buy fresh vegetables and meat, and they would cook them the same day. Fresh. Fresh. Fresh. We would never eat frozen food. This commitment to freshness wasn't just a preference, it was a way of life, deeply ingrained in our culture and daily routines.

One of my favorite memories is of the abundance of seafood available to us. Conch was right from the sea and was always at the marketplace. Squid, too. I loved eating all the seafood. The flavors were incomparable, the textures, a delight to the palate. Each bite was a reminder of the bounty of our island nation and a connection to the Caribbean waters that surrounded us.

But it wasn't just seafood that made our meals special. As for the goat meat, we didn't have goats in our yards. We just bought their meat at the market. This highlights an important aspect of Haitian culture and economy that I grew to appreciate more as I got older. In our culture, there are people who grow vegetables and raise the goats in the mountains, and then they sail them down to Port au Prince. That's how we get them to the marketplace. This system of local production and distribution was the lifeblood of our community. It ensured that we always had access to the freshest ingredients while supporting the livelihoods of our fellow Haitians.

As I grew older, I began to understand that this emphasis on freshness and quality wasn't just about food, it was a metaphor for life itself. The care and attention we put into our daily meals mirrored the care and attention we were expected to put into all aspects of our lives.

My childhood wasn't just shaped by the flavors and rhythms of daily life in Haiti. It was also profoundly influenced by the complex dynamics of my family. In addition to my five siblings, my father had some other children as well —maybe three more, a sister, and two or three brothers. This extended family added both richness and complexity to my young life, teaching me early on about the intricacies of human relationships and the importance of adapting to different situations. But the sibling I was closest to was my brother, the fourth one born. He was just so much like me, and we went out and did things together all the time. Later, when I was older, he would be the first of the siblings I would bring to New York after I moved there.

However, the stability of my childhood was shaken when I was eleven years old. It was then that my father separated from my mother, leaving a void that I, as the eldest child, felt compelled to fill but also "required to fill," by virtue of me being the firstborn child and inheriting a cultural responsibility. Can you imagine five of them running after me, and me after them? It made me grow up very fast.

This sudden thrust into responsibility was a turning point in my life. Overnight, I went from being a child myself to being a caretaker, a role model, and a second mother to my younger siblings. The weight of this responsibility was heavy, but it also ignited something within me: determination, resilience, and a work ethic that would serve me well in the years to come and all through my life.

Part II: The Birth of a Seamstress

It was during this tumultuous time, at the tender age of 13, that I discovered my true calling—sewing. The story of how I started sewing is one that has shaped the course of my entire life.

One day, my mother was supposed to come back from doing her business and make a dress for me to go to the neighborhood Christmas party. But as the hours ticked by and my mother didn't return, I realized I had a choice to make. I could either miss the party or take matters into my own hands. Without hesitation, I chose the latter. I thought about the task at hand, figured it out, cut the dress, sewed the dress, and ended up making the entire dress all by myself! I was 13 years old. What made it so remarkable is I had no formal training, no guidance, no pattern to follow. No one ever showed me how to sew. There were no sewing classes in school.

But the dress I created that day always holds a special place in my heart. It was a yellow gingham pattern, in beautiful yellow and white colors. I can still draw the dress, even after all these years. That simple act of necessity—creating a dress so I could attend a party—turned out to be the first stitch in the tapestry of my life's work. This is how my sewing business started.

Even today, I look at many of my creations and often ask myself, "How did I do these things?" I just figure out how to do it and then just "go and do it." And of course, God helps me; He is the primary source. Until this day, I give God credit for guiding my hands.

The response to my homemade dress was overwhelming. After the holiday when school re-opened, all the girls in my school went crazy when they saw my dress that I had sewn.

The excitement of my classmates was contagious, and soon I found myself taking work orders to make clothes for all the other girls and they paid me! Oh my God! I had more orders than I could handle. So, every Saturday after that was spent making clothes for other people; I was a born entrepreneur starting from the age of 13. I had to make the dresses and school uniforms for every girl and all their party dresses too, and they all paid me for my work. At this time, when I was 14 to 16, everybody who had money dressed all the time, so I had to make many of their dresses for multiple occasions.

It wasn't just my classmates who were impressed. Word spread quickly through the neighborhood, and soon girls from all over were asking me to make their dresses too. I charged 20 cents each, which was equivalent to 1 Haitian Gourde in the early 1960s and at that time was considered a decent amount. Looking back, I can see now that this was the beginning of my entrepreneurial journey.

However, not everyone saw my newfound passion as the blessing I knew it to be. My father had very different plans for my future. He didn't put much faith in a "career in sewing." He wanted me to become a medical doctor and go to medical school.

This desire wasn't just about ensuring a stable future for me—it was deeply rooted in cultural expectations. Being the "1st Child" born, it was expected that I would be and do something very special; it meant being the best I could be. And in my father's mind that was becoming a doctor. The patriarchal figure really doesn't care what you want; that's not important. Even if they don't take care of you, the father still wants you to be a doctor.

However, as my skills improved and my reputation grew, I found myself juggling more responsibilities than ever before. This was a very hectic time for me because I am still a teenager going to school full-time, and sewing every weekend, and through my paid work I'm giving my mom money to take care of us. Luckily, I had an uncle, my mom's brother, who also used to help out my mother. In a way, maybe he also influenced my brothers as a male role model.

Our Haitian culture taught us many important values. Even as young children, we were taught to be responsible and to care for people. My culture and the early responsibility of caring for my siblings made me mature early. Playing games like other kids? Never, never, never. There were always too many important things to do for our family.

I'm always working. Always working. Always. All my friends are going to dances, but I'm making their clothes for them. But me? No time for that. But I tell you, it wasn't hard for me. It was a pleasure. I was always doing it. I often joke that if I am addicted, my addiction is "working"; like some people are addicted to drinking or smoking, mine is just "working."

Yet, my teenage years weren't all work and no play. When I turned 16 or 17, I had a boyfriend, so on Sundays, we would go to the beach, you know, a family thing—but not every Sunday, just once in a while.

Despite my busy schedule, I loved school. I especially loved History, French, and Literature. These subjects influenced my life and inspired a love for history that would later inspire me to travel and learn as much as I could about the history of people and their countries.

My high school years also brought an important figure into my life, a boyfriend who was not only a romantic partner but also an intellectual mentor. He was a poet, a writer, and was also my teacher. He was an intellectual and saw my worth.

However, life in Haiti during my teenage years wasn't without its challenges. The political situation in the country was becoming increasingly unstable, creating an atmosphere of uncertainty and fear. Corruption and instability under Papa Doc's presidency made life challenging. It was no secret; it affected everyone, young and old.

It was in this context that I, like many young Haitians, began to look beyond our borders for opportunities. Around the age of 17, I decided to move to America for better opportunities. This wasn't an easy decision—leaving behind everything and everyone I knew was daunting. But I saw it as a necessary step to secure a better future for myself and my family.

At a friend's prompting, I applied for a U.S. visa through a program at the American embassy for people with trades and was accepted. The choice was a fortuitous one for after a time, they called and gave me my green card in Haiti. There were no additional tests or questions to answer, but the green card sat in my house for six months because the next question arose, "Does my boyfriend come with me?" His answer was no; he just wanted me to go and then come back once I got my papers. But when I answered, "I got to go back to New York so I can bring my mom and my siblings and bring them to the States also." His response was given reluctantly, "Okay. Get your citizenship, and then you come back." I told him, "Yes." But I knew I wasn't going to come back until I had everybody in New York, and that's exactly what I did. This acceptance to go stateside was a pivotal moment in my life. It represented not just an opportunity for me, but a chance to change the trajectory of my entire family.

The night before my departure to America was filled with a mix of excitement and anxiety, but a last-minute complication could have derailed my plans entirely. Previously, I had made plans to stay with a friend in New York, who assured me, "Oh, you can come and live with me." So, the night before I left Haiti, I decided to confirm I had a place to stay and call this friend. In these times, in our growing but humble country, not every house had the luxury of a telephone, so we used to go to a place called Teleko where they had a booth with a phone. The process was interesting. You would go into the booth, the operator would then place the phone call for you, and when the person on the other end answered, the operator indicated you should pick up the phone. I waited…but the operator never told me to pick up. Finally, I opened the door to the booth, and she told me, "Come out." And then she said, "When are you leaving?" I said, "Tomorrow." The woman continued, "You don't have another place to go?" I answered, "No." She responded, "Well, your friend in New York didn't answer." (But that wasn't true. The friend did answer but she told the operator, "Tell her you didn't find me at home.") But this news did not deter me; always the optimist, I returned home.

STITCHING DREAMS

I relayed what had transpired to my mother. Remember, this is the evening before my flight is due to leave Haiti. Quite concerned, my mother queried, "What are you gonna do?" My answer was simple and without hesitation, I said, "I am going."

My mother, bless her heart, stayed up all night worrying about my situation. In the morning, she acted. She approached a relative and got the address of a cousin in NY, which she gave to me on a little piece of paper. This act of love and support from my mother gave me the confidence I needed to take this leap into the unknown.

I kept that piece of paper hidden safely in my purse, not knowing that it was the only key I had to a haven when I arrived in a new world. When I boarded the plane to America, a young woman who had never been away from her homeland, I was not fully aware of the wealth that I carried with me: the skills, values, and determination that I had learned in Haiti and had been instilled in me by my family and the traditional culture of my heritage. These values and skills would be my inner and outer tools that would sustain me as I carved out a new life in a new world, threading the needle of my destiny with every stitch.

CHAPTER 2: STITCHING A NEW LIFE IN AMERICA (AGES 21-30)

I arrived in New York on August 17, 1970, at the age of 21. The journey from Haiti had been a whirlwind of emotions and new experiences. As the plane descended toward JFK airport, I couldn't believe my eyes. I had never been out of Haiti before, and I had certainly never seen such massive buildings. The sprawling cityscape below me was like something out of a dream—or perhaps a beautiful nightmare.

After landing, I managed to hail a taxi outside the airport terminal. The driver loaded my single suitcase into the trunk as I climbed into the backseat, still in a daze from the long journey and overwhelming sights. As we drove, I stared out the window in amazement. We crossed over the largest, longest bridge I had ever seen in my life, the Verrazano-Narrows Bridge, though I didn't know its name at the time. The sheer scale of it boggled my mind.

Finally, the taxi came to a stop on a busy street corner. It was at the corner of Broadway. As I got out of the cab, my eyes rose to see the tallest buildings I'd ever seen, and they were lining both sides of the street. To this day, I still remember what the cab driver said to me as he set my suitcase on the sidewalk. He said, "Good luck," and then he was gone in an instant. I think he meant it; his words were not gruff, but maybe New Yorkers don't show their emotions like they do in Haiti. People rushed past me in all directions, paying me no mind. The noise, the crowds, the frantic energy—it was all so different from the Haiti I knew.

And there I stood. All I had was a piece of paper with an address clutched tightly in my hand—the address my mother had given me at the last minute before I left Haiti. But in the next moment, fate intervened in the form of a young Haitian man passing by who noticed my lost expression amongst the bustling street passersby.

"You just came?" he asked in English.

He nodded and asked where I was going. I showed him the address on my paper, and to my great relief, he recognized it. "Oh, Max! I know him. Let me take you," he offered kindly.

He led me through the hustling streets to an apartment building where my cousins lived. When we arrived and knocked on the door, my cousins were shocked to see me. They had no idea I was coming. Despite their surprise, they welcomed me into their home, providing a much-needed haven in this overwhelming new world.

As I settled in over the next few days, the reality of my new situation began to sink in. I was in America now, and I needed to find work quickly if I was going to survive and build a life here. cousins made that very clear. While I could stay with them initially, I would need to find my own place soon. "You left your mother and your father in Haiti," another one of my cousins told me frankly. "Now you are an adult. You need to find a place to live."

Their words were a reminder of the responsibility I now carried. I couldn't rely on my family to take care of me indefinitely. If I was going to make it in this new country, I would have to be self-sufficient. With renewed determination, I would set out to find a job and a place of my own.

Just three days after arriving in New York, one of my cousins took me to the Robert Hall clothing factory in Brooklyn. "You have to work," she told me. "You have to send money back home to your mom in Haiti." The pressure was on, but I was ready for the challenge.

When we arrived at the factory, I was immediately intimidated by the massive industrial sewing machines. They were unlike anything I had ever worked with before in Haiti. But I was determined to prove myself. When they asked if I knew how to use the machines, I replied confidently, "I can learn." And I did.

They decided to give me a chance, starting me on a simple task—sewing head sleeves onto men's suit jackets. I threw myself into the work, determined to succeed. That first day, I managed to complete 300 jackets. I was elated, certain I had impressed my new employers with my speed and skill.

However, my bubble quickly burst when I noticed the woman working next to me, a Greek immigrant named Maria. She was like a machine, her hands flying as she worked. To my 300 jackets, she completed 1000. I realized I had a lot to learn if I was going to keep up in this fast-paced environment.

"Little girl, work!" Maria scolded me. "Don't look at me, work!"

I took her words to heart, keeping my head down and focusing intently on improving my speed and technique. The work was challenging, but I was grateful to be earning money —about $4 to $5 per hour, which, at the time, seemed like a fortune to me. Each week, I would send a portion of my earnings back to my mother in Haiti, fulfilling my promise, especially as the oldest, to help support my family.

Now that I was working, but I also needed to find a place of my own to live. I was fortunate to find a room to rent for $15 per week from a kind Jewish landlord named Sam. This was my first real home in America, a small space but one I could call my own. Sam's kindness and understanding were a blessing during those early days when I was still finding my financial footing. There were times when I struggled to make rent, but Stan was always patient and compassionate.

"You're a good girl," he would tell me. "Money is good, but people are good too. You can pay me next week."

His words and actions showed me that there were people willing to extend a helping hand to a hardworking immigrant trying to make her way. Stan's kindness made a lasting impression on me and helped ease some of the loneliness and challenges of those first months in a new country.

The factory job was just the beginning of my journey in the American workforce. As I became more comfortable with the industrial machines and the pace of work, I began to look for opportunities to advance my skills and my career. I knew that to truly succeed in this new country, I would need to continue learning and growing.

In the evenings, after long days at the factory, I began taking classes at the Fashion Institute of Technology (FIT). I paid for these classes myself, seeing them as an investment in my future. The instructors quickly recognized my natural talent, but they were also refreshingly honest with me.

"You don't need a degree here," one teacher told me candidly. "Just connections."

I found that I often knew as much, if not more, than many of the other students. Years of practical experience in Haiti have given me a solid foundation in sewing and garment construction. In fact, I frequently ended up teaching my fellow students, sharing the techniques and skills I had developed over the years. One instructor even confided that the other students preferred my methods to those being taught in class.

As much as I valued the education I was receiving at FIT, I realized that my real strength lay in the hands-on experience I had gained through years of sewing. The instructor's words about connections resonated with me, and I began to focus on building relationships within the industry.

After my time at Robert Hall, I worked various showroom jobs, each one helping me to hone my skills and build my reputation. These positions exposed me to different aspects of the fashion industry, from patternmaking to garment construction to client relations. I absorbed everything I could, dead set on mastering every facet of the business.

My big break came when I landed a job at Vogue Patterns. For the next ten years, I immersed myself in the world of high fashion, writing sewing instructions and checking patterns before they were sent to be printed in Altoona, Pennsylvania. This experience was invaluable, giving me an insight into the technical aspects of patternmaking and garment construction that would serve me well throughout my career.

STITCHING DREAMS

Working at Vogue was a dream come true for a girl who had started sewing dresses for her friends in Haiti. Every day, I was surrounded by the latest fashion trends and techniques. I took pride in ensuring that each pattern was perfect before it went to print, knowing that seamstresses across the country would be following my instructions to create beautiful garments.

During these years, I was not only building my career but also putting down roots in my new home. After five years in the United States, I applied for citizenship, proudly becoming an American citizen. This was a significant milestone for me, a tangible symbol of how far I had come since that day I arrived in New York with nothing but a suitcase and a dream. (I had returned to Haiti to see my boyfriend, but as expected, he had no desire to come to the US and advance himself. That did not deter me.)

Becoming a citizen also allowed me to fulfill a promise I had made to myself when I first arrived—to bring my family to America. I was able to sponsor my mother and siblings to join me in New York. Watching them arrive and settle into life in America filled me with a sense of pride and accomplishment. I had not only built a life for myself in this new country but had also been able to extend that opportunity to my loved ones.

As I approached my late twenties, my personal life began to evolve as well. I met a nice man, though, at the time, neither of us was interested in marriage. At 29, I gave birth to my son, followed by my daughter when I was 34. I chose to raise them as a single mother, a decision that came with its own set of challenges but also immense joy and fulfillment.

STITCHING DREAMS

My children's fathers did not offer financial support; I didn't need it. I was making the money I needed to support my children and my family.

The priority of education was instilled in me as a child, and I was determined to give my children the best opportunities possible. I enrolled them in a private school in Manhattan, working tirelessly to afford the tuition. It wasn't easy, but I believed a strong education would set them up for success in life. Seeing my children thrive in school, I felt a sense of pride and accomplishment. This was why I had come to America—to create a better life, not just for myself, but for the next generation.

Throughout these years, as I balanced work, motherhood, and continuing education, I never lost sight of my goal—to have my own business. I knew that true success and independence would come from being my own boss, creating my own designs, and building my own brand.

In 1983, after leaving my position at Vogue, I finally took the leap and opened my own business. It was a risk, but an opportunity presented itself and I felt ready to strike out on my own, armed with the skills, experience, and connections I had cultivated over the past decade. I had learned not just how to sew and create patterns, but how to navigate the complex world of the New York fashion industry.

Starting my own business was both exhilarating and terrifying. I was an entrepreneur at 13; it laid my foundation but now there were many sleepless nights as I worried about making ends meet, fulfilling orders, and building a clientele. With each successful project and each satisfied customer, my confidence grew. I established a reputation for quality work and innovative designs, drawing on my Haitian heritage and the skills I had honed in New York.

CHAPTER 3: WEAVING SUCCESS: MY FASHION EMPIRE (AGES 30-50)

The skills and connections I'd built over the past decade in New York's fashion industry had prepared me for something bigger. In 1983, after leaving my position at Vogue, I took the leap and opened my own business. Now, I was ready to expand further.

An opportunity arose when I learned about a small factory for sale. I approached a friend and asked to borrow $20,000 to buy it. It was a substantial sum, but I felt in my heart that this was the right move. The factory was located on 35th Street between 7th and 8th Avenues, right in the heart of New York's Garment District.

We started small, with just 15 employees, but word spread quickly about the quality of our work. Soon, we were producing garments for many of the top fashion houses on 7th Avenue. Our specialty was women's clothing—shirts, blouses, skirts, pants, and even bras. No job was too big or small for us to tackle.

As the business grew, so did our team. Eventually, we expanded to 28 employees, including some of my brothers who I had brought over from Haiti. They helped with various tasks, though interestingly, only my first brother who came to NY had inherited the family "gift" for sewing. He became an invaluable asset, always ready to help with the most intricate sewing work. We named the factory H & R, a combination of my name, Herla, and my brother's name, Reynor.

To expand our client base, I put an ad in Women's Wear Daily, advertising that we did small production runs. This strategy paid off as we started getting orders from well-known labels like Flora Nikroos and Norma Kamali, particularly for their women's negligees.

While the production work for other labels was steady, I felt a pull to create something of my own. The inspiration came from an unexpected source—my young daughter, Kimarah. I had always made special dresses for her, and without fail, other mothers would stop me to ask where I had gotten such beautiful clothes. When I told them I made the dresses myself, they would inevitably exclaim that I should sell them.

That's how the idea for Kimarah, my children's clothing line, was born. I decided to focus on exquisite party dresses, drawing on my love for pastel colors, delicate fabrics like lace, chiffon, and organza, and intricate details that made each piece feel special. Our first exhibition was at Penn Plaza, and I was amazed by the response. Buyers and boutique owners flocked to our booth, eager to place orders.

It was at this show I met Naomi Jacobson, an experienced sales representative who offered to represent my line. With her help, we soon began selling to major retailers like Saks Fifth Avenue and Bloomingdale's, and over 70 specialty boutiques across the country. We also participated regularly in Jacob Javits' trade shows and organized trunk shows to showcase our designs directly to customers.

Our dresses quickly became popular for special occasions, particularly bar and bat mitzvahs. We even set up a showroom where Jewish women would come to buy directly for these events. The mothers appreciated the delicate designs and high-quality craftsmanship that made their daughters feel special on these important days.

One of my proudest moments came in June 1988 when Essence magazine featured one of my dresses in a Father's Day spread. Seeing my creation in a national publication was a tremendous validation of my work. It proved that my designs could compete with the best in the industry.

As the business continued to grow, I found myself traveling to trade shows across the country. We exhibited regularly at the Jacob Javits Center in New York, and I even flew to Dallas one year to show our line. My daughter Kimarah would often accompany me, serving as both a model and a natural-born salesperson. Her charm and enthusiasm were irresistible to potential buyers.

Back at the factory, we were constantly innovating and expanding our offerings. In addition to the children's line and production work for other labels, we began taking on more specialized projects. One exciting job came when we were asked to make pants and shirts for Michael Jackson's background singers for a show. We completed the work and sent it to California, thrilled to be associated with such a major star.

I also developed a particular knack for creating elaborate bridal and evening gowns. Word spread quickly in New York's tight-knit immigrant communities, and soon I was the go-to dressmaker for diplomats' wives and other international clientele. I made clothing for ambassadors' wives at the UN, not African-style apparel in the traditional manner, but creating European-inspired designs that they preferred.

This connection to the diplomatic community led to an interesting opportunity. Some of the African delegates' wives asked if I would be willing to travel to their home countries to teach sewing skills to local women. They explained that while there was bountiful talent and beautiful fabrics in places like the Ivory Coast, many sewers lacked the specialized techniques for 'finishing' that European fashion demanded. Young people would visit Paris to learn these techniques and bring them back to Africa, implementing their new skills with the beautiful, colorful African fabrics.

I ran the factory in New York for about five years, from 1985 to 1990. As the 1980s ended, I found myself at a crossroads. The Kimarah line was thriving, but managing both the children's wear and the custom gown side of the business was becoming increasingly challenging. After much consideration, I made the difficult decision to move my business to Florida in 1990.

The transition wasn't without its hurdles. I continued to participate in Jacob Javits' shows after the move but initially struggled to find skilled workers in Florida. It took time to assemble a team that could meet my exacting standards. These labor challenges, combined with changing market dynamics, eventually led me to phase out the children's line.

However, this challenge led me to refocus on my business. I began specializing in bridal wear, making every kind of bridal gown imaginable, including dresses for the mother-of-the-bride and the entire bridal party. Clients would bring me pictures of $10,000 wedding gowns, and I could recreate them for just $3,000. This ability to provide high-quality custom designs at a fraction of the cost became a cornerstone of my Florida business.

Thanks to a referral, I also began a long-lasting relationship with a mega icon, Disney, making costumes for their shows and characters in both their cruise lines and theme parks. This partnership has now lasted for 20 years and continues to be a significant part of my business.

In Florida, I also expanded into religious garments, making nuns' habits, priests' vestments, and even choir gowns. This diversification allowed me to use my skills in new and meaningful ways.

Throughout this period, my faith remained a cornerstone of my business philosophy. I often prayed over my work, especially when tackling particularly difficult projects. I truly believed that my talent was God-given, and I had a responsibility to use it to bring beauty and joy into the world.

CHAPTER 4: DESIGNING DREAMS: MY WORK WITH DISNEY (AGES 50-PRESENT)

As I approached my mid-fifties, I never imagined my career was about to take a magical turn. My decades of experience in the fashion industry had prepared me well, but nothing could have fully readied me for the whimsical world of Disney costume design. It all began in 2004 when I was 56 years old. A small, unexpected job would open the door to a partnership that has now lasted nearly two decades and allowed me to showcase my skills on a truly grand scale.

That first Disney contract came out of the blue. I remember the day clearly—I was working in my shop when I got a call from a woman named LaQueen. She explained that she worked for Disney and needed someone to execute a design for her. A mutual acquaintance had recommended me to her. I was intrigued but didn't think much would come of it initially.

I met with LaQueen and helped bring her design to life. She was impressed with my work and apparently sang my praises to her boss, a man named John Doty. "John, I see you sending work everywhere," she told him. "There's a woman here in Orlando. This woman is so good. You will not believe... She's a designer. She had a line of clothes in New York."

STITCHING DREAMS

A few weeks later, LaQueen called me again. "Herla, spell your full name for me," she asked. I obliged her, not thinking much of it. Then she requested my social security number and federal tax ID. That's when I realized something bigger might be in the works. "Just wait for a call," LaQueen said cryptically before hanging up.

She later told me she had felt divinely inspired to go upstairs to the executive offices that day and fill out a vendor application on my behalf. "I'm sitting at my desk. I heard God—He told me to go to the upstairs office, get an application, and fill it out for you," she explained. Whether it was divine intervention or simply good timing, I'll never know for sure. But I do know that call changed the trajectory of my career.

My first official Disney job was decidedly unglamorous—they needed 40 garment bags made. But I was thrilled, nonetheless. The bags were for carrying costumes between the theme parks and cruise ships. At $66 per bag, the total came to $2,640. It wasn't a fortune, but it was a foot in the door with one of the world's most beloved entertainment companies.

I threw myself into the work, determined to impress. My brother, ever supportive, reminded me this was just the beginning. "Now, you're excited doing this?" he asked incredulously when I told him about the job. "But you are worth more than that." I simply smiled and said, "I am in Disney. My feet are in! Don't worry."

Those first garment bags were just the start. Slowly but surely, more work began coming my way. Small alterations here, a few costume pieces there. With each completed job,

Disney's trust in my abilities grew. Before long, I found myself creating elaborate costumes for some of their most iconic characters and popular shows.

One of my favorite early projects was working on costumes for the Aladdin show. The rich, jewel-toned fabrics and intricate embroidery transported me to a whole new world of design possibilities.

As my reputation within Disney grew, so did the complexity of my assignments. I began working on costumes for other beloved shows like Frozen and Pirates of the Caribbean. Each production presented its own unique challenges and opportunities for creativity.

The Frozen costumes were particularly memorable. I remember working on Elsa's iconic ice-blue gown. The intricate details and the way the fabric flowed were truly special. It was a challenging but rewarding project, knowing how much joy these costumes would bring to the performers and audience members alike.

But of all the characters I've had the privilege to create, Mickey and Minnie hold a special place in my heart. I like to make Mickey and Minnie because, you know, they are the stars. There's something eternally charming about those classic silhouettes people all over the world know and cherish.

Of course, working with such iconic characters comes with a great deal of responsibility. Disney is understandably protective of their images. I quickly learned the importance of discretion and confidentiality in this line of work. While I'm allowed to discuss the shows I work on, the specific character costumes are off-limits. It's a small price to pay for the joy of bringing these beloved figures to life.

My work for Disney isn't limited to the main character costumes. Over the years, I've created all types of accessories—gloves, shoe covers, bloomers, and corsets. Each piece, no matter how small, plays a crucial role in bringing the overall vision to life. I take pride in every detail, knowing that even something as simple as a perfectly fitted glove can make all the difference in a performer's comfort and confidence.

One of the most challenging—and rewarding—aspects of my Disney work has been creating costumes for their cruise ship productions. These shows demand costumes that are not only visually stunning but also practical for the unique conditions of performing at sea. Fabrics need to be durable yet lightweight, able to withstand the humidity and constant movement without losing their shape or color.

In 2021, at the age of 72, I embarked on what would be my most intense Disney project yet—a 21-day job on one of their cruise ships. This wasn't a vacation cruise by any means. From dawn to dusk, I was hard at work, altering costumes, training the onboard seamstresses, and solving any wardrobe emergencies that arose.

The days were long, and the work was demanding. I'd start at 7:00 a.m. with a quick breakfast, then head straight to the sewing room. Fittings, alterations, more fittings—the cycle seemed endless. Many nights I didn't finish until 9:00 or 10:00 p.m. There were moments when exhaustion threatened to overwhelm me. I remember one particularly grueling night, turning to the crew and declaring, "This is modern-day

STITCHING DREAMS

slavery!" We all shared a much-needed laugh before diving back into our work.

But even in those challenging moments, I never lost sight of the magic we were creating. Watching the performers take the stage in costumes I had lovingly crafted, seeing the joy on the audience's faces—made every long hour worth it. And truthfully, I was in my element. This is what I was born to do.

These days, my Disney work continues to be a significant part of my business. I have two full-time seamstresses working with me now, both of whom I've personally trained in the specialized techniques required for costume work. Their skill and dedication allow us to take on larger projects and meet the often-tight deadlines that come with show business.

One recent exciting project has been creating costumes for Disney's newest cruise ship, the "Treasure." The work is steady and demanding but incredibly fulfilling. I feel a sense of pride knowing that my creations will be part of creating magical memories for families from every corner of the world.

Of course, my work with Disney hasn't entirely eclipsed my other passions. I still create custom bridal gowns, mother-of-the-bride dresses, and outfits for entire bridal parties. There's special satisfaction in helping a bride find her perfect dress, often at a fraction of the cost of designer labels. Women will bring me pictures of $5,000 gowns, and I can recreate the essence of the design for just $3,000. It's not about undercutting other designers; it's about making dreams accessible to more people.

I've even expanded into creating vestments for priests and other religious garments. It's deeply meaningful work knowing that my creations will be part of sacred ceremonies and traditions. Whether it's a Disney costume or a priest's robe, I approach each project with the same level of dedication and attention to detail.

My partnership with Disney has been a true blessing, allowing me to stretch my creative muscles and work on a scale I never imagined possible. But it hasn't always been smooth sailing. The work can be demanding, the deadlines tight, and the standards exacting. There have been moments of frustration and exhaustion along the way.

One memorable encounter during my Disney work was with Ben Vereen, the famous tap dancer and actor. He needed last-minute alterations to his costume for a Disney performance. I quickly made the necessary adjustments. A few days later, I received a beautiful thank you card and a potted plant from him. The card said, "Thank you for making my life very good!" That plant, nearly 30 years later, is still thriving in my home.

My role has evolved over the years. While I still do hands-on work, much of my time is now spent supervising and training my team. I take great care in teaching them the specialized techniques required for costume production. It is keeping the beautiful art of sewing alive.

CHAPTER 5: STITCHING FAITH AND FAMILY

My story as a mother began in New York, where I found myself raising two children on my own. It wasn't easy, juggling the demands of a growing business with the responsibilities of single parenthood but my faith, my Haitian culture, and my family have been the foundation of my success and happiness. They gave me strength and my children gave me purpose. I poured everything I had into providing for them and creating a stable, loving home.

From an early age, my children showed distinct personalities and ambitions. My daughter, always articulate and persuasive, declared her intention to become a lawyer. My son, with his analytical mind, set his sights on becoming a brain surgeon. I encouraged their dreams, knowing full well that children's aspirations often change as they grow. After all, my own path had taken unexpected turns.

While neither of my children inherited my passion for sewing, my daughter displayed a natural talent for sales that emerged in the most charming way. As a little girl, she would often accompany me to trade shows, modeling my dresses with grace and confidence beyond her years. I recall one show where she captivated everyone's attention. As people admired her dress, she would smile brightly and say, "Oh, you like this?

STITCHING DREAMS

My mom made it! You should buy it for your store. We offer all sizes. Go to booth number..."

Her sales pitch was irresistible. Buyers would chuckle at her precociousness, but they'd also follow her directions straight to my booth. She had an innate understanding of how to connect with people and showcase the product. I often joke that she sold more dresses than I did on those days.

As my children grew, I was keen for them to maintain a connection to their Haitian roots, particularly through language. My daughter showed an interest in speaking Creole, our native tongue. While she doesn't speak it fluently, she makes a concerted effort to try, which warms my heart. My son, on the other hand, speaks Creole quite well. This is largely due to a decision I made when he was a teenager to send him back to Haiti for a time. There, as a boy growing into manhood, he would have plenty of family to guide him and keep a watchful eye.

It wasn't an easy choice, but I felt it was necessary. New York, for all its opportunities, also presented many distractions and potential pitfalls for a young man. It was important to reconnect with his Haitian heritage and the values that I held dear. They have been my faithful, ingrained roots which I wish to pass on to my children. The time he spent in his home country had a profound impact on him, strengthening his grasp of Creole and deepening his understanding of our culture.

Today, my children have grown into adults I'm immensely proud of. My son lives just six minutes away from me, a fact that brings me great comfort. He's incredibly protective, always checking in on me. It's become a family joke—if I don't pick up the phone by the fourth ring, he's at my door, worry etched on his face. "Mom," he'll say, exasperated but loving, "you want to kill me?" I'll laugh and reply, "With what?"

My daughter, ever the independent spirit, has made her life in New York. But distance hasn't diminished our bond. She FaceTimes me multiple times daily, always eager to share her day or seek my advice.

In addition to my children, I've had the privilege of raising my granddaughter, a truly special girl, who has brought so much joy into my life. From the moment she came into my care, I was determined to give her every opportunity to succeed. I sent her to Catholic schools, believing in the value of a faith-based education. She thrived there, participating in the choir and developing a strong moral foundation.

When it was time for college, I was overjoyed when she received a full scholarship to Florida State University. She chose to study entrepreneurship, a path that seemed her natural calling and filled me with pride. Perhaps some of my business acumen had rubbed off on her after all!

To celebrate her high school graduation, I took her on a Mediterranean cruise. It was a magical experience, exploring ancient cities and creating memories that will last a lifetime.

My faith has always been the cornerstone of my life, guiding my decisions and inspiring me to use my success to give back. This was never more apparent than on my 75th birthday. I wanted to celebrate this milestone—three-quarters of a century!—in a special way. I invited all my family to join me for a grand celebration on the beach in

STITCHING DREAMS

Cancun at an all-inclusive resort. The setting was magnificent, with a private pool in the backyard.

As we gathered on the beach that day, surrounded by the people I love most in the world, I received a phone call that would touch my heart deeply. It was from a pastor I knew, calling to share some extraordinary news. He told me about an article he had written titled "The Power of a Seed." The "seed" he referred to was a donation I had made 19 years ago, after much prayer, to open a sewing center in Bihar, India.

I remember that decision vividly. I had been moved by the stories of women in India who lacked opportunities for education and employment. Sewing changed my life and gave me independence and success. I felt called to share that gift.

Now, years later, this pastor was calling to tell me how that small seed had grown. The sewing center in Bihar had flourished beyond my wildest dreams. It had expanded to 99 locations across India, training over 2,200 women in the art of sewing. These women were now able to support themselves and their families, breaking cycles of poverty and dependence.

But the impact went beyond just economic empowerment. The pastor shared that 40% of the women trained in these centers had converted to Christianity. While this was never my intention—I believe everyone must find their own path to faith—I was moved by the idea that these women had found hope and purpose through this program.

As I listened to the pastor's words, as tears of joy streamed down my face; I was struck by the magnificent ways God works. A small act of generosity, inspired by faith, had rippled out to touch thousands of lives.

This experience only deepened my commitment to giving back. In addition to supporting the sewing centers in India, I also send monthly support to a school for children living on the streets of Haiti. My heart aches for these children, who grow up in dire circumstances. I can't help but think of my own childhood in Haiti, of the opportunities that allowed me to rise above my circumstances. If I can play even a small role in providing similar opportunities for these children, I feel compelled to do so.

My efforts to give back and contribute to my community haven't gone unnoticed. In 2008, I was deeply honored to receive the Martin Luther King, Jr. Good Citizenship Award. Dr. King's message of equality, justice, and the power of service has always resonated with me. To be recognized with an award bearing his name was humbling.

Following this recognition, I received a letter from the Florida State Senate, congratulating me on the award and acknowledging my contributions to the community. The letter read, in part: "Congratulations on receiving the 2008 Martin Luther King Junior Good Citizenship Award. Best wishes for continued community service and outstanding citizenship."

These accolades, while deeply appreciated, have never been my motivation. I simply strive to live out my faith and to use the talents God has given me to make a positive difference in the world. This ethos was beautifully captured in a feature article about me in the Catholic newspaper, which dubbed me "God's Seamstress."

The title touched my heart. Throughout my career, I've always felt that my ability to sew was a gift from God.

STITCHING DREAMS

Whether I'm creating a costume for Disney, a wedding gown for a bride, or vestments for a priest, I approach each project with reverence and gratitude. Each stitch is a form of prayer, an expression of thanks for the talents I've been given and the opportunities I've received.

CHAPTER 6: THREADS OF ADVENTURE: MY TRAVELS AND CULTURAL EXPERIENCES

Throughout my life, the art of sewing has been my constant companion, weaving together the fabric of my experiences. But as I've grown older, I've discovered another passion that complements my love for needlework—travel. My journeys around the world have not only enriched my life but have also provided endless inspiration for my work. Each trip is like adding a new, vibrant thread to the tapestry of my life, creating a rich pattern of cultures, histories, and spiritual encounters.

One of my most profound travel experiences has been my pilgrimages to Medjugorje, a small village nestled in Bosnia-Herzegovina, bordering Croatia. This tiny place speaks to my soul, and I've been blessed to visit this sacred village three times—in 2021, 2022, and 2024. Each visit has left an indelible mark on my soul, strengthening my faith and providing moments of profound spiritual connection.

During my visit in 2021, I decided to take on the challenge of climbing to the top of Apparition Hill, where the Virgin Mary is said to have appeared to six local children in 1981. The climb was no easy feat, especially for someone my age. It took an hour and a half to ascend and another hour and a half to descend. But oh, the view from the top! I have a cherished photograph of myself at the summit, holding a red flag that proudly declares, "Jesus is the King." The sense of accomplishment and spiritual elevation I felt in that moment is something I'll carry with me always.

That trip was made even more special because I was able to share it with my daughter. Together, we visited the statue of the "Weeping Christ," a powerful symbol of divine sorrow and love. I remember standing before it, overwhelmed by its significance. What I didn't realize at the time was that my daughter had climbed back up to the statue after we had left. Someone captured a video of her praying there, touching the water that flows from the statue. When I saw that footage later, my heart swelled with joy. It was an answer to my prayers—to see my child connecting with her faith in such a profound way. It was something I had always wished and prayed for.

These pilgrimages are always undertaken with a special group of people, fellow seekers who share my deep faith and curiosity about the world. There's something truly magical about experiencing these sacred sites together, sharing in each other's wonder and reverence.

My travels have taken me to Rome twice, a city that never fails to inspire me with its rich history, spiritual significance, and exquisite art. Each visit to the Eternal City feels like stepping into a living museum of faith and art. I've had the privilege of visiting Assisi twice as well, walking in the footsteps of St. Francis and marveling at the simplicity and beauty of his teachings. And, of course, how could I leave

STITCHING DREAMS

Rome without purchasing beautiful fabric God has something in store for me to make.

In September 2023, I embarked on an ambitious pilgrimage that took me to 11 different cities. This journey was a whirlwind tour of Catholic history, with each stop revealing new wonders. We visited countless churches, each one a testament to the enduring power of faith and human creativity. I was struck by how the frescoes adorning the walls and ceilings of these ancient buildings looked as fresh and vibrant as if they had been painted yesterday. It was as if time had stood still within these sacred walls—preserving God's history.

One of the most memorable stops on this tour was a visit to "The Church of the Relics." As I stood before the relics of saints like St. Luke, I felt a deep connection to the long and rich history of my faith. It was like stepping into heaven itself, surrounded by these tangible links to the holy men and women who had come before us—preserving the greatness of God's saints forever. I found myself captivated by each relic, each story, each piece of history that is awe-inspiring within those hallowed walls.

Another highlight of my travels was visiting the Basilica of Saint Anthony in Padua. The reverence and devotion I witnessed there was truly moving. Pilgrims from all over the world came to pay respects to this beloved saint, and being among them, sharing in their faith and hope, was a powerful experience.

Of all the cities I've visited, Florence holds a most special place in my heart. There's a romance to Florence that's hard to put into words—it's in the air, in the architecture, in the art that seems to be around every corner. I was in awe of Michelangelo's works, especially his extraordinary statue of David. Standing before it, I couldn't help but marvel at the skill and vision that could turn a block of marble into something so lifelike and powerful. The works of Leonardo da Vinci were equally inspiring, reminding me of the limitless potential of human creativity.

Rome, of course, offered its own treasures. The Sistine Chapel left me speechless—how could I possibly describe the beauty of Michelangelo's ceiling? It's one thing to see it in pictures or on television, but to stand in its presence, craning my neck to take in every detail, was transformative.

The Colosseum was another highlight of my time in Rome. On my second visit, I was fortunate to have an excellent guide who brought the history of this ancient amphitheater to life. Learning about the gladiatorial contests and the tragic fate of many early Christians within those stone walls was sobering. It made me reflect on the strength of faith those early believers must have had, to face such terrors for their beliefs.

My trips have also taken me to Pisa, where I saw the famous Leaning Tower. It's one thing to see pictures of it, but to stand before it, to see how it truly does lean at such an improbable angle is mind-boggling.

One of my most cherished travel memories is my visit to Venice in 2023. It had been a lifelong dream of mine to see this unique city built on water, and the reality did not disappoint. Gliding through the canals on a gondola, I felt as if I had stepped into a painting. The play of light on the water, the centuries-old buildings rising on either side; it was magical.

During my time in Venice, I also visited the island of Murano, renowned for its glassmaking. Watching the skilled artisans at work, transforming molten glass into delicate, beautiful objects, was fascinating. It reminded me in many ways of my own craft—the patience, skill, and attention to detail required to create something beautiful.

My love for textiles often influences my travels. Near the Church of St. Nicholas in Italy, I stumbled upon a fabric shop that was a treasure trove of beautiful materials. I couldn't resist buying some, my mind was already racing with ideas for new creations inspired by the colors and patterns I saw there.

One of the most profound moments of my travels came in Vatican City. As I stood in St. Peter's Square, I felt as though a miracle was happening! I found myself incredibly close to the Pope's vehicle, known as the Popemobile, so near that I could almost reach out and touch the Holy Father himself. At that moment, I was overwhelmed with emotion. Here was I, a girl from Haiti, standing in the heart of the Catholic Church, mere feet away from the Pope...successor of St. Peter. It felt like a miracle, a testament to how far faith and determination had brought me.

The churches of Rome never ceased to amaze me. The frescoes that adorned their walls and ceilings were like windows into history, telling the stories of saints and sinners, of faith and struggle in exquisite renderings. Each church held its own treasures, its own stories, and I found myself wanting to linger in each one, soaking in the atmosphere of reverence and awe.

Not all my travel experiences were equally enjoyable. Of course. I visited Pompeii but found that I "wasn't too crazy about it." Perhaps it was the stark reminders of mortality, or maybe it just didn't resonate with me as other historical sites did. Travel, I've learned, is as much about discovering what doesn't move us as it is about finding what does.

Sicily, on the other hand, was a delight. Seeing the Mount Etna volcano was overpowering. It made me reflect on the magnitude of nature and the resilience of the people who have lived in its shadow for centuries.

Malta was another memorable stop on my travels. I visited a church that was said to be built on the site where St. Paul was jailed after his ship was wrecked on the island. The anchor from his ship is preserved in a museum there. Standing in that place, I felt a connection to the early days of Christianity, to the struggles and triumphs of those who spread the faith across the ancient world.

My journey to Jerusalem was truly a spiritual homecoming. Walking the streets where Jesus walked, seeing the places mentioned in the Bible—it made the scriptures come alive in a way I had never experienced before. I had the profound experience of entering Christ's tomb and Lazarus' tomb. The weight of history and faith in those moments was most overwhelming.

Not all my travels have been purely religious in nature. I've also had the joy of experiencing some of the world's great cultural events. In Cannes, I attended the Children's Book

STITCHING DREAMS

Festival, a feast for the imagination. Seeing the creativity and passion that goes into creating stories for young minds warmed my heart. I also visited Marseilles, soaking in the vibrant atmosphere of this historic port city.

One of my most treasured travel memories is the Mediterranean cruise I took with my granddaughter. It was a celebration of her high school graduation, and what a celebration it was!

As mentioned, for my 75th birthday, I decided to create an exceptional memory, gathering my entire family for a celebration in Cancun and the beach was just steps away. Surrounded by my loved ones, and the sound of the lulling waves in the background, I felt wholly blessed. It was a perfect way to mark three-quarters of a century of life, love, and adventure.

My passion for travel shows no sign of slowing down. In 2024, I went on a 13-day Pilgrimage to Lisbon, Fatima, Salamanca, Avila Valle de los Caidos, Segovia, Burgos Lourdes, and Barcelona. This was a spectacular trip. We visited the Church of St. Stephen/Church of the Holy Miracle, home to the 13th-century Eucharistic Miracle. I also spent a whole day in Avila, home of Saint Teresa and the Carmelite Reform. While in Avila, I took a tour to Valle de los Caídos, Valley of the Fallen, which is an underground church. On another day, I spent a day in Lourdes, Barcelona, and visited the Sagrada Familia and the mountains of Montserrat.

Each of these destinations holds its own allure—the melancholic beauty of Lisbon, the vibrant energy of Barcelona, and the timeless elegance of Paris. I can't wait to

STITCHING DREAMS

see what new inspirations, what new threads these places will add to the tapestry of my life.

And my travel dreams extend even further. I've long harbored a desire to take an Alaska cruise. The idea of seeing the rugged beauty of the Last Frontier, of witnessing glaciers and fjords, of possibly seeing the Northern Lights—it all fills me with excitement. It's a reminder that no matter how much of the world I've seen, there's always more to discover.

CHAPTER 7: THE ART OF BALANCE: MARTIAL ARTS AND WELLNESS

Never in my wildest dreams did I imagine that at 76 years old, I'd be practicing martial arts five days a week. Yet here I am, at the end of each workday, immersing myself in the ancient disciplines of Tai Chi and Kung Fu. This unexpected journey began in late 2020, born out of a practical need but blossoming into a passion that has reshaped my golden years.

I started practicing martial arts in late 2020, at the age of 72. My initial motivation was practical—I was preparing for a pilgrimage to Croatia that would involve climbing mountains. "I have to strengthen my legs," I thought, "and have to be good to go." I needed to improve my overall fitness for this challenge.

I began taking classes in Tai Chi and Kung Fu at a local studio. To my surprise, I found myself enjoying the practice immensely. What started as preparation for a trip quickly became an integral part of my daily routine. Now, at 76 years old, I practice martial arts five days a week.

The benefits of my martial arts practice became apparent quickly. It helps me relax and takes away the stress from my work and deadlines. Tai Chi, with its slow, graceful movements, helps me find a sense of calm and balance. Kung

STITCHING DREAMS

Fu, on the other hand, provides a more vigorous workout that challenges my strength and agility.

I've made significant progress, reaching the fifth level in my training. This achievement feels particularly special given that I started this journey in my 70s. Recently, I was even featured on my martial arts studio's website, demonstrating moves for potential new students. Seeing myself in those photos, executing moves that would have seemed impossible to me just a few years ago, is a powerful reminder of how far I've come.

One of the most noticeable improvements has been in my balance. Through regular practice, I've developed the ability to stand on one foot "forever." This improved balance isn't just useful in class; it helps me in my daily life, too, making me feel more stable and confident as I move through the world. Learning "to breathe properly" helps me gain access to the "spirit of life itself." I feel so much more alive and well when I am breathing deeply and getting in touch with the energy of my soul. I practice proper breathing techniques throughout the day. When I'm feeling stressed or the need to focus, I often find myself using these breathing exercises to center myself.

My martial arts practice has become part of my lifestyle. I make sure to practice at the end of each workday. It's become a ritual that I look forward to, a way to transition from the demands of work to the peace of the evening. During these sessions, I often find myself laughing as I move through the forms. There's joy in the practice that I hadn't expected, a sense of playfulness that complements the discipline and focus required.

STITCHING DREAMS

Recently, my instructors asked if I could make uniforms for them, combining my sewing skills with my new passion. I'm currently working on taking their measurements and designing the uniforms. It's exciting to bring together these two important parts of my life—my lifelong career in sewing and my newfound love for martial arts.

At 76, martial arts practice helps me maintain my energy and health. It keeps me moving, keeps me challenged, and keeps me engaged with life. Each class is an opportunity to learn something new and push myself a little further. I'm often asked how I maintain my vitality at my age, and while a healthy diet and my work certainly play a role, I credit much of it to my martial arts practice.

The impact of martial arts on my life goes beyond just physical fitness. It's taught me perseverance, the importance of continuous learning, and finding balance—not just in standing on one foot, but in all aspects of life. As I face the challenges that come with aging, I feel better equipped to handle them, both physically and mentally, thanks to my martial arts training.

In many ways, my approach to martial arts mirrors my approach to life and my work as a seamstress. It requires patience, attention to detail, and a willingness to continually refine and improve. Each movement in Tai Chi or kung fu, like each stitch in a garment, contributes to the whole. And just as I take pride in a beautifully finished piece of clothing, I feel a sense of accomplishment with each new skill I master in martial arts.

CHAPTER 8: PRESERVING THE ART: MY LEGACY AND VISION FOR THE FUTURE

At 76 years old, I'm still working and have no plans to retire. The concept of retirement doesn't exist in my world. I often tell people I never see "retirement" in the Bible. For me, sewing is not just a job; it's my calling, a way of life I can't imagine ever giving up. My fingers are still nimble, my eyes are still sharp, and my creativity flows as freely as ever.

Every day, I ask God for the energy to continue my work. It's a simple prayer, but it's what keeps me going. Some mornings, I wake up feeling every one of my 76 years, but as soon as I sit at my sewing machine, those aches and pains fade away. My passion for sewing is as strong as ever, and I'm always looking for ways to improve and inspire my craft. And I have a passion and dedication now—to passing on my love for sewing and preserving this beautiful dying art form.

I find myself drawn to documentaries on art and history, particularly those focusing on costumes and special occasion dresses. These programs feed my creativity and often influence my designs. I might see a gown worn by a queen in the 18th century and think about how I could adapt that style for a modern bride. Or I'll watch a documentary about traditional African textiles and get inspired to incorporate some of those patterns into my work. It's a constant process of learning and growing, even after all these years. However, they are also a source of constant nourishment and inspiration for the mind, body, heart, and soul. They feed and inform my senses of the uniqueness, greatness, and beauty of every culture on earth, and inspire my love of travel to see, understand, and witness as much of life as I can.

Recently, I've taken on a new challenge that brings me great joy— teaching a 16-year-old boy the art of sewing. This young man has what I call "the Gift"—that innate understanding of fabric and form that can't be taught, only nurtured. Watching him work reminds me of my own early days at the sewing machine and reinforces my belief in the importance of passing on this craft to the next generation. His enthusiasm is contagious, and it reminds me of why I fell in love with sewing in the first place.

I often encourage young people to embrace sewing as an art form. In a world of fast fashion and disposable clothing, there's something magical about creating a garment with your own hands. I want the younger generation to understand the value of this skill, not just as a hobby, but as a potential career path. When I see the pride in my young student's eyes as he completes a difficult seam or masters a new technique, I know I'm doing my part to keep this art alive.

Looking back, I do have one regret. When I was younger, I had an opportunity to intern in Paris at haute couture houses. A client who was impressed with my work suggested it, but at the time, I couldn't see myself leaving New York. I was just starting to establish myself, and the idea of uprooting my life seemed impossible. Now, I advise young people to take such chances when they come. You never know where they might lead. Who knows what I might have learned, what connections I might have made if I had taken that leap? My friend had told me, "You would live if you had to work in a restaurant, but you would learn things you could have never thought possible interning under the tutelage of the grand houses of haute couture fashion."

Despite that missed opportunity, my passion for sewing has never waned. I'm always looking forward to new projects. Currently, I'm working on creating an Etsy shop for communion and christening gowns. It's a project that allows me to use the expensive European fabrics I still have from my days of creating children's clothing lines. These fabrics are like old friends, reminding me of past creations and inspiring new ones. There's something special about knowing that these beautiful materials will be used to create garments for such important moments in a child's life.

Throughout my career, I've been blessed to work with multiple generations of families, creating wedding dresses, bridesmaids' gowns, and special occasion outfits. Each piece is a labor of love, and I firmly believe it's a collaboration between my skills and divine inspiration. I always know that God gave me this talent, and I don't take any pride in what I'm doing. Instead, I see each garment as a gift, a way to bring beauty and joy into someone's life. Sometimes, I'll meet someone who tells me I made their mother's wedding dress, and now they want me to make theirs. It's a beautiful continuity that I feel privileged to be a part of.

STITCHING DREAMS

When I'm working on a wedding gown, I always ask God to "put the last touch" on it. It's my way of acknowledging that while I may do physical work, the true beauty comes from a higher source. I've lost count of how many times I've stepped back from a finished gown, amazed at what I've created, knowing that it wasn't just me—it was God working through me.

I would like to elevate fashion to a standard of elegance. When I see a young person today enter church in short shorts, or a woman dress haphazardly, I want to grab them and say, "Let me dress you. Let me show you, it takes so little to look your best..."

Most of all, as I look to the future, I'm filled with a sense of purpose. I want to capture the beauty of sewing and its impact on my life. But more than that, I want to ensure that this art form continues to thrive. I'm concerned about the lack of skilled sewers in younger generations, and that's why I'm so committed to teaching and encouraging young people to take up sewing. It's not just about creating clothes; it's about understanding design, developing patience and attention to detail, and connecting with a tradition that spans generations back to our 1st ancestors.

My journey with sewing has taken me far beyond my wildest dreams. From a young girl in Haiti to a successful businesswoman in America, from creating children's clothing lines to designing for Disney—each step of the way has been guided by my love for sewing and my faith in God's plan for me.

STITCHING DREAMS

Now, as I look ahead, I'm excited about a very special trip I'm planning for 2025. I'll be visiting the "1st Sewing Center" in India, a project that I helped fund years ago. It started with a small donation--it's all I had but as always God provided, and over the years, that small seed has grown into something beautiful. The center has expanded to multiple locations, training thousands of women in the art of sewing. It's a powerful reminder of how a small act of generosity, inspired by faith, can ripple out to touch countless lives.

I'll be meeting women whose lives have been changed by learning to sew, just as my own life was transformed by this skill. It's a chance to see how the art of sewing, which has given me so much, is now providing opportunities for others. I wonder what their stories will be, what dreams they've been able to achieve through sewing. Are there women who have started their own businesses? Who have been able to provide for their families? Who discovered a passion they never knew they had? Who made creations through their hands they never thought possible? Some started businesses, and others started sewing centers.

This upcoming visit to India feels like a culmination of my life's work in many ways. It's a reminder that our actions can have far-reaching consequences, often in ways we never anticipate. I'm filled with gratitude for the path my life has taken, for the opportunities I've had, and for the chance to share my passion with others—a skill that has brought me so much joy and success is now doing the same for others halfway around the world and keeping alive an exquisite skill handed down by our 1st ancestors first to keep us warm and protected and then to adorn ourselves and enrich the universe with its beauty. It is a human art form, performed by the hands God gave us to create beauty in the exquisite fabric of our lives. I give you this precious Gift, learn it well and pass it on and you will be surprised at the standard of beauty you will create and the joy you will bring to the world!

www.ingramcontent.com/pod-product-compliance
Lightning Source LLC
Chambersburg PA
CBHW050735010526
44107CB00010B/858